# Find Your Fabulous

## Love Yourself on the Inside
## Look Great on the Outside

# Debra Shoults Bettendorf

I would like to thank my family and friends for always believing in me and showing me a lot of love.

Thank you to my publisher, Bob and Fran of Biblio Publishing for believing in my vision for *Find Your Fabulous* and embracing its uniqueness.

A big thank you to J.E. Berry for the beautiful endorsement!

I am so grateful to Mindy Drayer for writing a heartfelt forward for the book.

A very special thank you to Dr. Robert Lawson for his guidance and support through the entire process!!

ISBN: 978-1-62249-628-0

Published by
Biblio Publishing
Columbus, Ohio
BiblioPublishing.com

Dedicated and
Gifted to A Fabulous Person

To: _____

From: _____

# Endorsements

Find Your Fabulous, is without a doubt an outstanding piece of work that will encourage its readers to not only dress in style but to find their best selves in the process. The advice you share is powerful and life-changing. Self-talk is indeed a critical component to one's success in life. Thanks for reminding us that one's perception of oneself is paramount to what hurdles can be overcome.

Dr. Robert L. Lawson

"Who doesn't need a positive word to carry them through the day? In Find Your Fabulous, Debbie has given us snippets of grand positivity! Each page is like a dose of love from a close friend, or a nudge in a good direction from a favorite aunt. Debbie has let us sit close to her as she whispers encouragement to us through her creative writing. What a fun loving read!"

-J.E. Berry (Author, Speaker, Business owner)
Author of "The Truth About Happiness"
& "Set Free to be Set Apart"
JEBerrySpeaks.wordpress.com
JEBerrySpeaks.com

# Foreword

What is the one piece of clothing EVERY woman should have in her closet? What is the best piece of advice you can give your child? These are topics from one spectrum to another. Or are they?

*Find Your Fabulous* is a well-written, creative and engaging book that somehow combines the love of fashion with the love for life. Debra Shoults Bettendorf uses her professional career of fashion consultation to offer you, the reader, advice on how to dress for an interview to how to dress for fun and everything in between. But she doesn't stop there. So much of what people see on the outside can often reflect what is on the inside. Learning to accept yourself is the first step in developing a better YOU! Find Your Fabulous is a delicate way of reminding all of us how to get the most out of life.

There is one constant theme throughout the entire book. It won't take you long to figure it out. Do yourself a favor and read Find Your Fabulous. Once you turn that first page, it may be hard to put down. Thank you Debra for writing such a brilliant book that we all can learn from.

Mindy Drayer
Mom/Wife/Daughter/Sister/Friend
Author
Radio and TV Personality

*My mission in life is not merely to survive, but to thrive; and do so with some passion, some compassion, some humor, and some style.*

-Maya Angelou

I have used this quote many times. I believe that during our short time passing through this place called earth we should make the most of it. I don't believe in judging others; I believe it is important to be kind and I believe it is imperative for our own happiness to build up others. I enjoy seeing others succeed and feel good about themselves. It rubs off and is healthy for our own soul.

Love to laugh, love to have a good time and be silly. Sometimes we can take life too seriously. The style part of the quote is important too. Own your style and take a little time for yourself to dress in a favorite outfit even if you don't have time to get all done up...it makes us feel better when we do.

What is fabulous? Owning your $#!+. Be You and continue to grow as a person in positivity, love and light. Reject negativity, including negative self talk. Be the authentic and fabulous person you are meant to be.
I was hesitant to write a book but have kicked fear's ass and went for it. I am proud of myself and hope that the messages on these pages inspire you to be you, love yourself, own your $#!+ and be fearless in life. One life, Live it.

-Find Your Fabulous

# Lucy

Meet Lucy. She is a combination of the strong and beautiful people I have in my life all rolled up into one. I bet you can find yourself in her. I wrote this book for all of you. Enjoy reading this book of positivity with a dose of fashion. It will be fun gifting this book to special women in your life.

Lucy has curly red hair and is the sweetest person but don't anger her because she will not refrain from confrontation. She enjoys having fun and is the life of the party. Lucy likes meeting new people and learning about them because she is truly interested. She most generally will not stay in touch with the new people she meets but she appreciates them in the moment. This gal is intelligent and witty with great comebacks and jokes during conversation. She is definitely an asset to every party and there are no awkward silences with Lucy there. She believes in supporting other women and being their cheerleader. She will be a friend who will root for you, laugh with you (occasionally laugh AT you), cry with you and pray with or for you. She will defend a friend and her loyalty runs deep. You can tell Lucy anything and she will never repeat it. She loves to take walks and better for her if someone joins her because she likes to chat while she is walking. She will come at you with a barrage of questions and sometimes doesn't wait for the answer before asking another. She has lived long enough to realize that life is short and she wants to live life and enjoy every minute. She has been known to tell others "Don't let your Monday ruin your Sunday." Lucy is fashionable who appreciates a great outfit and loves shoes. She is the best for setting up girl time to continue to nurture friendships. She believes that time with her friends is the perfect outlet to let loose and have fun. She has been hurt by friendships in the past where she invested her feelings but has moved on and values those in her life with all of her heart. If Lucy hears music, she will dance. Don't even play Thriller by MJ or she will be sure to bang out the entire routine for her own entertainment, but of course everyone loves it. She enjoys the arts and a good concert. She had an appreciation for art at a young age. She enjoys a good book and is an eloquent writer. Lucy is a good cook and isn't afraid to take over the grill and make a great dinner. She is witty and can be a wise cracker but doesn't have a mean bone in her body. She is extremely empathetic and feels deeply. She has experienced deep loss and has powered through because she is strong.

Cheers to all the Lucies in your life.

# WELL HELLO FABULOUS, THIS IS MY WHY-

I have worked with women in fashion for several years. Over the years I began to realize even more than I already knew, it is NOT about the clothes. We have to feel good about ourselves on an inner level and then the clothes are a fun accessory. In working with clients, many times the session would move more toward discussions of being confident and accepting and loving their body. Fashion is fun but the only way to truly feel fabulous is to love yourself on the inside. To love yourself on the inside and be aligned with your heart and soul, know who you are and own it is when the magic happens. My son said something that resonated with me. He said that sometimes people can hear the same advice over and over and then someone else says the same thing in a different way, or with a different delivery and it makes an impact. My heart led me to write this book and my hope is that some of the messages will stick and help you FIND IT.

This book is a fabulous blend of heart and soul with a dose of fashion. It is filled with an abundance of positivity, charm and wit that makes it a great gift for you or any other fabulous woman in your life. You are never too young or too old to 'Find Your Fabulous.'

# Find Your Fabulous

'Just Because It's <u>IN</u> Style,
Doesn't Mean It's <u>Your</u> Style'

'Transforming into a more
beautiful you, inside and out'

'It is <u>NOT</u> about the clothes'

" Look at that wiggle worm
mommy "

" Yes, and soon that wiggle
worm' will become a
butterfly "

We are all on a journey
to transform into the most beautiful
version of ourselves on the inside,
and outside.

We want our inners as beautiful
as our outters — FYF

# Self • Love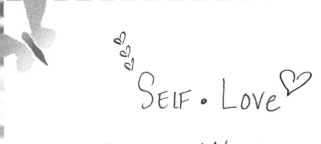

FIND IT !!! The absolute
Only way to find your fabulous
is to love yourself.

Loving yourself is not being conceited or selfish. Loving yourself is necessary to be able to fully accept yourself and be happy — find joy. ♡

You can dress up in a gorgeous outfit - but if you don't love yourself and have confidence then you won't be Owning it and looking as fabulous as you could look.

I have been known to say,
" You can dress up a turd, but it's still gonna stink! "

# WHAT ADVICE WOULD
# I GIVE HER?

I think my birthstone must be a seashell; I have always felt at home by the ocean. Looking through old photos and seeing this little girl I find myself asking, what advice would I give her? What would my future self tell her? A lot of years have been lived since this picture was taken on the beaches of West Palm where my Grandparents lived in fall and winter.

1. I would tell her to be confident
2. Be kind
3. Appreciate every day

One, I know that confidence does not come from someone saying, "Hey be confident" no more than telling a depressed person to "Hey, just be Happy." So if I am able to take my future self back in time to my childhood, then I am going to take her through some scenarios of life that I have lived with examples of times we could have been more confident. I believe that we are all on a journey to become a better version of ourselves and let's face it there is room for improvement in all of us, even with confidence. I truly believe confidence happens when you finally become who you are meant to be. The real you, the most genuine YOU. Even if that means the real you gets annoyed getting stuck behind someone who

walks too slowly or the real you talks a lot. Eh hem guilty of that and much more but I will own that for now.

Two, Be Kind. I believe my past self always knew that. I would chat with her and show her times that being kind wasn't the easiest thing to do, but being kind was the right thing to do. The only difference in this I would explain is, sometimes people to whom you are kind will see that as weakness or think you are ignorant. When someone is not nice to you and you choose to just be kind in return, it can lead them to believe that you are fine with the mistreatment, or you are too ignorant to understand that they are being unkind/mean to you. I would tell her to always be kind anyway. The problem is with them, not you.

You are not for everyone, and some people will not like you just because they don't want to like you. Don't change for anyone. Stay true to you. In high school I would downplay my strengths and even my intelligence so I could be more approachable or likable for everyone. I would try and be funny and put myself down for a laugh. If I have done one thing right, it was to talk with my children and encourage them to do the best they can in every area of their lives. Talk nicely to themselves and to be who they are and if someone doesn't like them then well...you are not for everyone.

Still, Be Kind.

Three, Appreciate every day. I can tell her with confidence that life has a way of getting away. Appreciate each day for what it is. Some days and some periods of time are going to be difficult but keep your head up and remember that you will get through it and be wiser from it. Start yoga NOW, meditate. Breathe. Take a minute to show gratitude for the things you have in your life. We have ONE LIFE. I would then grab her shoulders and shake her...one life, do you hear me? You can do anything you want to do. You are able and capable. One Life.

If this is encouraging to just one person who reads this, then it makes me so happy. WE have a voice and we can share our thoughts to encourage others and that is a beautiful gift.

What should I wear
to my event ?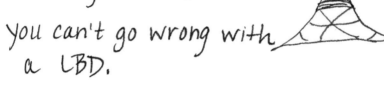

You can't go wrong with
a LBD.

Everyone should have a little
black dress in their wardrobe).

Invest in a classy LBD
that is made well and fits well.

POP OF COLOR

poppin' wha....

Popping Champs and
adding color.
Sometimes we just need to
add a colorful piece of jewelry
or shoes to give an outfit some
pop!

## MONOCROMATIC

Keeping it all one color is #1

Using one color top to bottom can be a beautiful thing.
It can make our body appear longer and leaner.

The most gorgeous outfit
is FABULOUS only if the person
wearing it OWNS it and is
confident.

Confidence Is GORGEOUS!

My Grandmother always
said, 'Waste not, want not'

So don't leave those sale
items you love on the rack!

Clearly this is not what
She meant. I hear her in my
head when I have to throw away
Spoiled food.

OH, and please RECYCLE

# Go Ahead and Dress Up....Just Because

Most of us gals can remember back to our childhood when we used to play dress up. We would have plastic heels and tiaras and maybe a few boas to wrap around our neck, and if we were lucky we had a tutu to prance around in. I used to love going to my grandmother's basement and getting into a huge barrel of clothes that she made up for me. She had scarves and skirts and heels and more. I had the best time and felt great.

I guess the point of this message is, we grow up but if we are all being honest with ourselves, when we put on a fabulous outfit (playing adult dress-up) it makes us feel good. I don't know the science of this fact, but there is something to it. Some days you may see me in the grocery store all dressed up and ask what I have going on that day. I may not have anything special going on but it just may be one of those days when I want an extra boost to feel fab.

I always like to say that it is NOT just about the clothes but rather how you feel in them. It may not be someone else's style, but it is your style and it makes you feel great. You will walk with confidence and own it. Confidence is gorgeous.

# FIND YOUR FABULOUS

What is YOUR fabulous?
Only you can find it.

We are unique and find joy
and give joy to others in
different ways.

Start by loving yourself first
so you can love others.

♡

Find it?
FOUND IT!

# HOLD UP!

I am trying to FIND
MY FABULOUS —

# Just Breathe

You don't have to be a full-time Yogi. Just breathe. Are you holding your breath?

Take some deep breaths in through your nose and let it out of your mouth. Let all the tension go with it.

Do this in your comfy yoga-wear or NOT! Just Breathe ☺

## It's About the Shoes

That's how Prince Charming found Cinderella afterall

An amazing outfit can be DESTROYED with the wrong shoes.

# Opt for Nude Pumps

Want to elongate your legs? Want to have your dress or other ensemble be the star of the show? Opt for nude shoes. Sometimes when we put on a pair of awesome shoes, it can compete with our dress or other outfit and it just doesn't do it for you. Okay, well try on a pair of nude pumps and look again. I love to wear my little black dress LBD with nude heels as well. Makes it look as though I have legs for days, and the focus is on the dress. (and legs)

Not saying I always wear nude pumps with my dresses, because I like to have different "looks' but if you want to keep it classy and fresh and aren't sure about what shoes to wear, go naked...I mean wear nude.

**p.s. there are many different shades of nude...ALWAYS select the color that best matches your skin tone.**

What KIND of person
are you ?

Be Kind. What you put
out in to the universe comes
back to you.

Be Kind while wearing
sweatpants or an evening gown —
JUST BE KIND —
BE NICE ♡

# ⊓ STAPLES

These staples don't come from an office stapler.

They are the pieces you select for your wardrobe that tie everything together. They are the classic pieces that stay when other trendy pieces go.

Some Examples:

* Great pair of jeans
* white button down
* well fitting neutral t.shirt/s (for layering)
* Black pants- fits well, your go.to
* Jacket- Blazer - neutral
* LBD

# SAME CLOTHES, DIFFERENT LOOK

Maximizing your wardrobe can be much easier than you think. I would guess that you have things hanging in your closet right now that you have never worn because you don't know how to wear them, where to wear them or just not sure how to put it all together. I like to show clients how to take their staples or "base" clothes as I call them and add new things to them for a different style and feel. Take your amazing black pants and add different shoes, top, jacket, sweater and change up the entire vibe. Switch it up a bit!

I like to add *toppers*. I have a great pair of black pants that I typically wear a nice black sleeveless top with and then add different blazers, jackets and jewelry to totally change the look.

SAME 'BASE' CLOTHES
ADD 'TOPPERS'
TO CREATE NEW LOOKS

Say nice things to yourself.

Build Yourself UP↗ like you do for others.

Be on T-E-A-M YOU ☺

Pack a pashmina (large scarf) in your handbag to grab for an easy and fashionable cover while on the plane. You can use it like a blankie and then quickly wrap around your neck when you jump up. They are great to use once at your destination as a shawl on an evening out OR even a swimsuit cover-up! I have used it multiple ways. :)

# MORE TRAVEL

Throw a few dryer sheets in your luggage.

It keeps clothes smelling fresh and ~~fabulous~~.

It also helps with static cling.

When you open your suitcase it will be like a burst of yummy fresh !

Use the dryer sheets beside the air conditioner and your hotel room will smell better too.

# Tea Time

## You are my cup of tea

A hot cup of tea in your favorite mug is a mood lifting, warm and cozy thing to do.

Trends are FuN
but they come & go.

Grab some trends to add
to your classics but
the more $$ items should
be those that you will have for
a few years. ☑

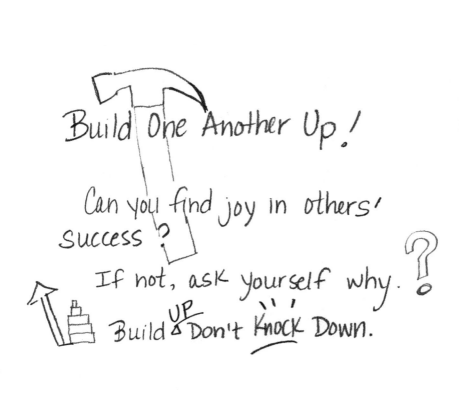

Build One Another Up!

Can you find joy in others' success?

If not, ask yourself why.

Build UP Don't Knock Down.

Build Your Outfit around your favorite pair of shoes.

Sometimes we get stuck over what to wear and using an item for inspiration can help. ☺

## Nature

Get out there and take
a walk. Kick off your fashionable
Shoes and feel the earth under
your feet.

Remember, you can not pour
from an empty cup. Give yourself
some time to refuel and fill your
cup up first. ♡

ツ

# TWO QUESTIONS
## LIFE & STYLE

1. Does it make you feel good?
2. Does it *fit* your personality?

I have been helping clients select clothes to compliment their body, going through their closets and playing finders keepers--losers weepers and also presenting to groups of people about dressing for their body type as well as what is appropriate interview attire.

It is said that science proves that getting it right with your appearance definitely has an impact on your overall attitude toward yourself and your productivity in your day.

The two simple questions above can be used for the outfit you select for a day, or it can be a little guide for other things in life. The outfit has to come off and you may not always be on point with fashion...but you still want to feel good.

1. Does the outfit make you feel good? Does your job make you feel good? Does your relationship feel good? Okay, so the outfit isn't nearly as significant as the others but try and answer the question to whatever your circumstance. Prior to walking out of your house, ask yourself, do I feel good in what I am wearing? Prior to taking a new job ask yourself, will

this job make me feel good? Is it a job I can stand behind and enjoy? In a relationship ask yourself, does this relationship feel good? Is this a relationship that I gravitate towards because it is a happy place?

2. Does this outfit fit my personality? It IS true that no one can do you, better than you! Make sure the clothes fit properly, of course, but own *your* style. I have said this before too...how many times have you observed a person in something that is totally NOT your style, but the person wearing it is confident and owning it and that makes you actually like the ensemble? Be you, you do it best. I have to share the fact that I always tell people that I have never outgrown the love of glitter. I honestly do really love shimmer and shine but I don't wear it from head to toe. I will add a little glam and glitz whenever possible though, adding in small doses. Does my job fit my personality? Are you in sales, but cringe at the thought of approaching a client to make a sale? Are you a social person, but have a job in an office with no windows or others around you? What is your niche, what is YOUR thing? What fits your personality? In a relationship, (be friendships or love interest) does the other person allow me to be me? Does the relationship fit me and who I am?

In life we ask people questions. How often do we ask ourselves these questions in order to *find our fabulous*? Have a conversation with yourself and perhaps makes some changes.

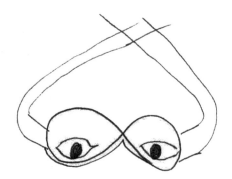

Self Doubt is like a
thief in the night stealing
all hopes and dreams and
opportunities for a bright future.

When self doubt breaks in —

PUSH IT OUT !

SAY NO !

~Debbie

Wear what makes you
feel FABULOUS and
Own It!

BOOM!

Confidence, like Vitamin D and exercise –

It does a body good!

My Grandmother told me that
a man that worked with her asked,

"Lois, how are you so kind to
me when I know how difficult I am?"

Her response —

"I pray everyday for God to
give me strength"

Ha, Ha.
He asked the question — and
he got the answer.

We can be kind even when it
isn't easy —

# Thoughts To Inspire

"It's not just about the clothes" and "Let your little light shine" and "Find inner beauty and it will radiate for people to see." I have said to clients, and I am saying to you because I believe it with my whole heart.

I want to share some thoughts;

My daughter loves to play volleyball, but she isn't very tall. She cannot will herself to grow several inches, but what she can do is play as hard and as smart as she can and be the best possible volleyball player she can be. She can be proud of her effort and of her improvements and not compare herself to others. We sure like to compare don't we? We are all guilty of it to some extent; It's called being human.

I hear people talk about being overweight or not being as pretty as someone else or how someone else is so lucky to have this or that. Once again, we all allow thoughts to creep into our head from time to time. I feel like some of the comments we make to ourselves are so rude that we bring ourselves down. Speak kinder to yourself. Okay, think I am crazy and I am the only one talking to myself? Be honest, how many times have you looked in the mirror and said," UGh, I look fat", or "When did I get all of these wrinkles?"

I just want all of my fashionistas who care enough to read this to remember, there's always going to be someone smarter, someone taller, someone thinner blah blah blah. We all have the ability to become the best possible versions of ourselves. Let your little light shine, wear the cute shoes, put on that outfit you have been saving for something special, speak kindly to yourself and I promise you will start to like yourself a WhOLE lot more. You are the only one like you, there isn't another (I am channeling Barney here), but this is true. Take care of you because there is no other like you.

There is greatness within you, even when you don't see it yourself.

# AGING

When you meet a person who is vibrant and full of LIFE –

They appear younger.

# AGING

Someone who doesn't think about the number of candles on their birthday cake and lives life and continues doing what they want and can, KEEP GOING.

We are all aging, so let us do so with grace and have fun! My Grandfather lived to be 95 years old and was active and mentally sharp. He would tell me to stay busy doing things I enjoy and to keep MOVING. He said that at his age there were days his body didn't feel like getting up out of bed in the morning, but he got up anyway because he knew that the next day he really might not be able to, so keep moving. He told me to read, do crossword puzzles, play cards and memory games because our brain needs exercise too. If you don't use it, then you lose it. By the time he was in his 90's he would brag to people about his age and people were shocked when they realized it. I think after a certain age, people continue to lie about their age but they start rounding up! He said he wanted to live to be 100 years old. He didn't make it, but my Uncle Wally had a 100th Birthday party for him anyway. Let me tell you, my Grandfather LIVED every single day of his 95 years. He was an amazing example to all.

He was so cute. He always dressed up and loved to be the center of the show. I remember stopping at the grocery store and from a distance I saw an elderly man who looked so handsome in his leather bomber jacket and cabby hat, and I realized it was my Grandpa.

You are the energy
in front of you — beside
you — behind you — all around
you !

Replace any negative thought
with a positive one.

Trees do not hang onto
their leaves when Fall Season
comes.
   They let them go.

   Change is Good.
                    —FYF

# MANAGING YOUR CLOSET

Getting control of your closet can be overwhelming after acquiring clothes over the years and the purchases of new items. Most of us have heard, "Out with the old and in with the new" but many times we hold on to everything and just add to our collection. All of a sudden, the closet is jam-packed and for some reason you feel like you have nothing to wear.

A few tips to help:

> * Before shopping, take a look at your closet and see what you actually need to bring outfits together or to give a new look to what you already have
> * When you bring home new clothes, try and get rid of the same number of items purchased
> * Don't keep clothes that you don't wear (sounds easy...I know it isn't...try)
> * Take out the clothes that don't fit. Don't stress, if you really like it just store it someplace else but it is in your way and taking up space that you need right now. (bet you take it out and you don't miss it and then you can donate it or take to a resale shop for extra $$)

Try some of these tips and hopefully it helps you get started to owning and controlling your wardrobe/closet and it not owning you. If you get super ambitious, turn on some fun music and pour yourself a drink and delve into your closet and organize!

When you buy a coat, jacket
or whatever, and the kick pleat is tacked
closed — PLEASE snip that. It is meant
to be open.

What to Wear Today —

KINDNESS & COMPASSION

Perfect Ensemble,

We never know what others
are going through —
It could be you who needs
others to be kind and Compassionate.

If your Light is
too bright for someone,
Tell them to wear
Shades♡

Dim your light
for No One !

─FYF

Have you skipped lately?

Skip and see if it makes you giggle.

I don't know what got into me one day, but I started skipping through the parking lot and it made me BELLY LAUGH!

Debbie Disclaimer—
Wear a sports bra

I always told my
Children to be themselves
and the people who are
attracted to you really
like You.

   If we aren't being our
true selves, then how would
we know who really likes
us. ?

Be Present, live in the moment. The past is over.

Same with style, allow your style to evolve and change with you.

# YOUR ENERGY AND YOUR OUTFIT

Just as your energy speaks to others before you ever open your mouth, so does your outfit. What does your clothes say about you? Are you holding on to pieces that do not fit you? Maybe they fit you but it is a style that doesn't compliment your figure anymore or it isn't your style for the person you are now. It is difficult sometimes to move onto a new style. You may be in a rut and are just used to wearing the same thing even though you don't feel amazing in it. If this is the way you are feeling, don't fret or feel overwhelmed. Try changing one thing in your wardrobe at a time to get you started. Maybe start with a new pair of jeans. Add a style that fits your body. Reach out to a stylist if you need to so you can get the help you need to acquire the best fit for your body. Once you establish what fits and compliments you the best, it will be easier for you to shop on your own.

PROGRESS $\longrightarrow$

<u>NOT</u>

PERFECTION

yeah – that !

How can you believe in anything IF you don't believe in yourself?

Find Your Fabulous

You have Guardian Angels

Always a fashionable
accessory.

They will never go out of style.

-FYF

Dogs know when you
are sad or stressed.
They walk over and sit
by you as if to say,
"Here, pet me, it will make
you feel better."
My son said dogs are like
a furry happy pill.
Dog spelled backwards
is GOD.
Thank you for giving
us dogs ♡

Shhh...

　　Listen –

We are human beings
and are flawed; however,
God made us and He doesn't
make mistakes.

　　You are beautiful. Continue
your journey of becoming the
best You.

　　( Read 3x )

# How To Dress For An Interview

I give presentations for college students on how to dress for an interview. I always remind them that while it would be wonderful for our interviewer to only see what we have to offer from reading our resume and our conversation, that is not the case. We are human beings and are extremely visual. In the first few moments of meeting someone for the first time, we start to make our impression. Everyone does this to a certain extent. Take the outfit out of the equation, don't wear something that will be a distraction from them getting to know you.

We all have our personal style and enjoy to some degree expressing ourselves through our clothes. I love trends like ripped and distressed jeans as much as the next person, but I would never wear them to an interview. My suggestion is keep it conservative. Have everything wrinkle-free, clean and closed toe shoes with minimal jewelry and little perfume.

Good Morning ~

Girl-Go Make Your
Bed —

Drink a big glass of
Water —

Have A Great Day !

# You Can Not Deny A
## Beautiful Heart ♡

Have you ever met
Someone who became even
more beautiful as you got
to Know them?

When someone judges you, it says MO_RE about that person than it does about you.

Stay true to you — Don't change yourself to please others.

XO

# Dress For Your Body Type

With all of the different styles that are available to buy, it makes it much easier to dress to fit your body type. I remember at different points in my life in fashion when you wouldn't be caught dead in a pair of wide leg jeans and then skinny jeans were a no no. Now we see a variety of styles to choose from in stores. There are an array of jeans from wide leg, skinny leg, boot cut, high waisted, low-rise, and on and on. Tops are available in awesome varieties of style as well. Cropped, long, hi-lo tops and the list goes on.

My tag line is, "Just because it's *in* style doesn't mean it's *your* style" What I mean by that is, I would rather wear something that fits me well and compliments my shape than wear something that is a fad that does nothing for me. Because there are so many styles "in style" right now, it makes it much easier to dress for your body type. Learn your body. It you have a little extra around the middle popping out (muffin top) when you zip your pants, you may want to choose a pant that is a little more high waisted, or you may need a larger size. Sometimes you may have to invest in a good seamstress if you have difficulty finding a size that fits you. If you buy the pant to fit your waist, then you can have the legs altered to fit nicely. If you already have pants that you love except you have "muffin top" then choose a top that doesn't cling to you, or put on a nice trimmed-in jacket to cover.

Going along the same topic, if you have extra in the middle then a great style of top is one that has ruching. It allows you to wear a shirt that is a little more form fitting and is flattering. I see women wearing tops that are way to big for them because they are hiding their middle, when in many cases it does the complete opposite by making them look bigger.

And remember to wear the correct undergarments...it can make a HUGE improvement with helping everything look smooth.

Say this Out loud
today –

I am Amazing

I am Fearless

I am Strong

I am Love ♡

Rinse & Repeat
ツ

Be who YOU are
Genuinely
Be your authentic Self.
We have unique gifts to
Share with the world !

Please Know that.
You don't Know what your
gifts are ?
Go within and ... FIND THEM !
FIND IT !

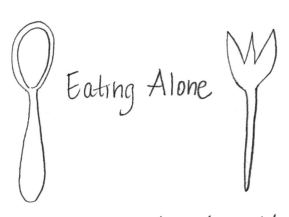

# Eating Alone

Years ago when I would go to a restaurant and see someone eating alone, I would feel sorry for them.

As we age and grow into ourselves we realize that time alone feels good. I was thinking about this one day when I was at a restaurant and said, "party of one." I sort of giggled to myself. "Wonder if someone feels sorry for me?"

I know who I am and I like being with me. I would have never gone to dinner at a restaurant alone in my twenties.

# YOUR MOTHER'S VOICE IN YOUR HEAD

MY MOTHER

I attended a 100th birthday party and was able to connect with friends I had not seen in a long time. During my visit with my friend Dawn, she said she had thought about me when she was doing some reading about "Finding Your Truth" and she thought that was sort of what I was trying do for my clients. As soon as that came out of her mouth I was reacting to the quote....think about it, Finding Your Truth. That is powerful. Then it "Dawned" on me. (sorry, I had to do it) I need to share some thoughts on the subject that Dawn and I discussed.

Good or bad, most of us have our mother's voice in our head. I know that most moms means well and want their children to be wonderful, successful and happy. Corrective criticism or honest opinions, however, can be misunderstood and taken in a different way and cause hurt feelings and some lifelong self confidence issues or hangups. My mom was super supportive and mostly complimentary but anytime she would say the slightest negative comment, it would stick. Now that I am a mother of two children, I not only hear my mother's voice in my head but somehow I have turned into my mother. Actually, she is amazing and I can only hope to be half the woman she is.

During my visit though....we discussed the fact that especially women have the resounding voice of their mothers in their heads and that isn't always a good thing. Sometimes that voice is hindering them from feeling confident in their appearance or feeling inadequate in some way. Find your inner voice, find your truth and drown out any negativity. I want to add that the voice in your head could be an aunt or grandmother or childhood friend. If their voice is in your head, I challenge you to hit the mute button and give yourself a compliment in its place. Try it. Be the best possible version of you....what is your truth? Find it. Own it.

Can We Just Discuss
Menopause for a sec?

WTH?

How is it that it is something
women go through but the word
begins with 'MEN' ???

HA·

Maybe it is putting MEN on PAUSE?

Whatever the case... It can be
tough. It can start much younger
than people realize. If you are
having trouble sleeping, gaining weight,
joint pain and brain fog and all of
your tests are coming back negative for
other issues —
        You should have a blood test
to check hormone levels.

    You will get through it. There
are treatments available for us now
that can help. *

♡

What is your purpose
in life?

Get to know yourself better
and find out what you're good
at AND pay attention to what
you enjoy.

I believe that is our
PURPOSE.

♡

"Mom, this is itchy!"

"Mom this dress is uncomfortabe."
HA!

"It's the price you pay
for FASHION!"
—FYF

Sometimes we just have to
wear it and get over it!

~ Stylish at Any Age ~

When I hear women say
they are too old to wear jeans —
Say Whaaa?

As we age our style will change
to compliment our bodies, but in
NO way should we sacrifice our
style for the number of candles
on our cake.

If it fits and you feel fab
in it — WEAR IT

# PROPERLY FITTING ATTIRE

Make sure your clothes fit properly. Sounds like a no-brainer but many times people have the most fabulous outfits but the fit isn't on point and it doesn't score well. Whether you are getting an ensemble for a charity event, gala, ball or even a job interview it is important to make sure the fit is nice.

Some helpful tips to tell if the fit is right....

Men
* If you are wearing a sport coat or jacket, the shoulder seam should come out to where your natural shoulder ends. If the seam is short, the jacket will bind and the material will look pulled. If the seam is beyond your shoulder then it is too big and will look sloppy.
* The length of the jacket is important as well. If your arms are

resting at your sides and the jacket material extends much longer than your hands then the jacket is too long. If the jacket is much above your hands then it is too short.
* Remember your dress pants should be the correct length as well. I suggest the length be long enough to have a nice break in the pant as it falls to the shoe. Never allow your dress slacks to drag the floor, and being too short isn't good either. Remember when getting your pants altered to bring along the shoes you will wear with them and have them on while getting fitted. Styles change on pant length. Just be sure to feel confident in trendy styles if you choose them.

Ladies
* The same is true with jackets for getting the right fit across the shoulders, but we have so many different styles and lengths that we are able to mix it up a little bit.
* With pants we have more options as well with skinny fit, trouser style

etc...but it is never a good idea to have pants dragging the floor. Depending on what you wear and the fit, you will wear the shoe that compliments that style accordingly.
* Ladies, when getting a cocktail dress or evening gown do not get caught up with sizes. Every designer has their own sizing and please go ahead and get the larger "size" and have it altered to fit your body. The dress will compliment you better and you will be more comfortable.

There is much, much more to share but this is a start.
You may even want to take a look through your wardrobe and see if you have some things that could be tailored for that perfect fit. It can make a huge difference in your appearance.

~ Be Your Best ~

Surround yourself with
people who also want you
to be your best.

Yes!

Just as you try and eat
healthy foods to nourish your body,
you should surround yourself with
positive people who love and support you.

Feed Your Soul Good Stuff ♡

I believe we are
what we tell ourselves
we are.

What are you telling
yourself ?
?

# Expectations of a FIVE YEAR OLD GIRL

I always picked my children up from school. I would stand outside of the door with a big smile. One day, I had stayed home all day and was SUPER cleaning my house. I had on sweats and didn't even brush my hair.

When the door flung open, and I was standing there wearing a smile, my daughter looked and then looked again. She then said when we got to the car, "Mommy, can you look pretty when you come to get me instead of a RAGAMUFFIN?"

Seriously? Ha! No pressure Moms

One of my friends said —
'Dude I am just lucky to get here'
Ha

# NOTHING TO WEAR

Do you ever go to your closet and just stare at it? You even say out loud, "Uhhh I have nothing to wear!" The full closet of clothes wants to scream back..."Hey, what about me?" Every fashionista or want-to-be fashionista does this from time to time. Plan ahead and find your outfit for work or play in advance. Avoid waiting until the day or morning of the event. What helps put an outfit together when you get stumped could be finding one item to inspire you. "Hmmmm, I have been wanting to wear these cute shoes or I haven't worn my favorite shoes in a while, or I have a statement necklace I love but have never worn." Then take the inspiration item and build an outfit around it! Sounds a little silly, but it has helped me put outfits together many times. It even allows you to create different outfit ensembles that you have never put together before. Give it a try!

# Love and the Absence of it -

Love yourself so you can love others AND you are open to receive it.

Give Love
Receive Love

# NO LUMPS AND BUMPS

Keep the lumps and bumps in your homemade mashed potatoes and wear a body shaper to keep everything smooth under fitted clothes. I can't say enough about under-garments. It can make or break an entire outfit. It is not so much about how thin you are, or you aren't, it is if everything looks smooth. Have you ever seen (and it has been me before) someone with the wrong panties or bra? You can't see the beauty of the outfit because stuff is popping out different places and it is a distraction. Go ahead and wear the granny panties or body shape wear...please do! Pull those suckers up and laugh about it...because your clothes will look fabulous on you, and no one will ever know. (ok...maybe someone will know) ha ha.

Just remember to wear the correct undergarments...pull everything in, smooth it all out and look Fabulous!!

# Create Your Own Fabulous Morning Routine

## This is mine ♥

- Shut that alarm off!

- Feet on floor and stretch your arms over your head (ahhh)

- Big glass of water

- Coffee with a shot of ground cinnamon and sometimes powder collagen and a tiny bit of unrefined coconut oil

- Turn on diffuser with rosemary and sage oil

- Alexa, turn on meditation music

- Speak out loud what I am grateful for

- 4 days—go exercise (Boxing / Boom)

✱ I make my bed most days if a little chihuahua doesn't look too comfy!

H2O

# Fabulous Head To Toe

Be fabulous in an outfit from head to toe! Remember to always put your best foot forward and have your feet moisturized and a nice pedicure before gracing an event with open toe and/or sling back shoes. I love shoes, and always tell people that the wrong shoe can ruin the look of an entire outfit. Even worse is to have on a fab pair of shoes without having your feet in shape. We can probably all admit that we have seen this before, or we ourselves have chosen a different shoe because our feet weren't ready to be revealed.

I really enjoy a good pedicure but let's face it, we can't always go get a pedi. I keep my feet in shape myself through the winter months with a good foot soak. You can get an array of different brands. It keeps your skin moisturized and soft through the dry winter months. After you soak, it is easy to slough off dry skin. I like to put on a good moisturizer and then I wear fuzzy socks around the house. (no dry or cracked heels)

Another tip I like to share is the fact that I know many people do not like how their toes/feet look and hide them away. Try and get your feet in shape with the info I have shared and then choose a polish that blends with your skin tone. Maybe try a nude polish slightly lighter or darker than your skin tone, or even a pinkish tone that blends. This helps your toes look nice while not drawing attention to them with a bright or loud color.

Don't deFEET the purpose of those awesome shoes....put your best foot forward.

I had a young woman who was a new mom recently tell me that she loves every stretch mark and her stretched out tummy. She said that she loves her body for giving her a child.

— Positive Body Image —
She has it figured out at a young age. ♡

# IT IS WHAT IS ON THE INSIDE
# THAT COUNTS

On a family vacation with my family including my parents and sisters, we of course dined out most every evening. I always like to ask the locals where we should eat as they usually know the great spots that may not be on vacationers' radar. One of my sisters wanted seafood for her birthday dinner and Fisherman's Corner was recommended by a local that goes by the name 'Coach'.

We got all dressed up and when we rolled up to the place I said, "This can't be it!" I then read the sign and realized indeed it was and exclaimed, "Oh my goodness, I made reservations to a trailer with a deck addition!'"

Guess what? It was the best and most delicious seafood ever and everyone enjoyed their meals. This was another reminder that IT IS WHAT IS ON THE INSIDE THAT COUNTS.

# Under The Clouded Mind

Under the clouded mind lies
beautiful thoughts of self

The clouded mind shadows
your natural beauty
Some days the clouds thin and
you see glimpses of your authentic
self
Doubt and fear like darkness
creep in bringing clouds

Look up. Believe. Accept
See with Clarity and
Out comes the Sun

~Debbie

# Layers

We are not one dimensional beings. We have layers...

Speaking of layers —

Remember your layers when transitioning from summer to fall and winter.

Layers are our friend. I like taking my summer tops and bringing them with me through fall by adding a cardigan sweater, jean jacket, blazer or a pashmina over it. If you get too warm, it is easily removeable.

– Drop your shoulders down and away from your ears.

– Unclench your jaw

– Take a deep breath and own the day.

# SIGNS

For starters, I don't consider myself religious, but I consider myself very spiritual. I believe in God, and I believe that we are all part of the universe that He created. I don't get caught up in what Religion one follows; I get caught up in overall energy and positivity that one possesses.

During the time when my daughter was applying for law schools last year, she was extremely excited to apply and also very nervous at the same time. She applied for a few but had her number one pick and prayed to be accepted. She had graduated from Ohio State and really wanted to be accepted into their law school as well. To jump right in without too much back story, she did Not get in. She was so sad and super down in the dumps. She came home and we talked it out. On her way back to Columbus, I called her and asked, "Do you ever talk to God, like out loud?" "Do you ask him to show you signs that you are on the right path and if something better is coming your way?" She told me that she prays but she doesn't just have random convos with God. I told her to just have a conversation.

An hour later she called me and she was completely freaked out. She had gotten to her apartment and went down to the lobby to retrieve her mail. Sticking out of her mailbox was a large envelope from Moritz College of Law (her official letter of rejection, but she had previously received an email of rejection). On the large envelope was a yellow sticky note and printed on it was, "F**k Moritz."

Keep in mind, no one knew she had been denied at that point and the lobby is locked to the outside.

This was a pretty bold sign. We may not always get signs that are so IN YOUR FACE, but we all do get signs if we are open to receive them. I told my daughter that her fiery personality needed a bold message like that to resonate. It definitely resonated with her.

Oh, and she got into Capital and they gave her a nice scholarship. She wasn't super excited with that even though it was great. Fast forward a few months. She went to Capital's orientation where the Dean spoke to them. She called me crying afterwards and said, "Mom, this is exactly where I need to be."

Do You Like Me?

CHECK YES OR NO

☐ YES

☐ NO

It's okay — it isn't your job.
Liking me is my job.

Liking Yourself Is an Inside
Job

♡

~ Love Yourself ~

## JUST SAY NO

It is okay to say, "no." Sometimes I believe we feel obligated to give, give, give. Over-giving can lead to internal dissatisfaction and even feelings of resentment. If you do not have the time, room in your schedule or you just don't want to do something then don't do it. Also, in relationships if you are the one giving and you get nothing in return, that feels deflating. Give yourself permission to stop giving. I do not mean to keep score in the way of remembering everything you do for someone with expectations of getting something in return. You will be able to discern the times when you need to have more respect for yourself and stop, with no ill intentions or anger. You still care but you care more about your own happiness and self respect.

Practice saying no and it will get easier with time.

Buy Yourself some
flowers today.
OR
Bring some in from
outside if you can.

You deserve it.

Enjoy

# MAKE A MALA

I went to a yoga workshop and part of the workshop was sitting in a circle with other yogis and we made a mala. A mala is a simple string of beads used to count mantras, prayers or intentions. A full mala contains 108 beads. We all received our beads and prior to stringing them we spoke good intentions into one bead for each person and gave it to them for their necklace.

I am not a patient person and stringing beads onto a fine thread was not exciting to me. I ended up enjoying it so much and what it all represented meant so much to me. I wear my mala proudly and love the special beads from others and their intentions.

# Happy New Year or New Day

I am still evaluating my life and how I can be a better person and listing all of the things I feel I could do better. I enjoy helping people look fabulous and putting together outfits for events. I love working with others in pursuit of a perfect ensemble and going through closets to decide what looks fab on my clients and what isn't doing them justice. I also love to visit with them as I do this. We can learn a lot about one another and ourselves when we work with appearances. I have been so fortunate to work with people who are just as beautiful on the inside. In fact, I find that the people who reach out to me are the ones who are gorgeous on the inside and may just need a little boost to bring that inner beauty to the surface.

As we begin a new year, or a new day let us enjoy the moment and continue to work on our "inners & outers" Every DAY can be the start of your new year of the new and improved YOU.

# Take Your Outfit For A Spin

When you are planning your outfit for a special event make sure you get everything from head to toe laid out and ready to go. Steam it if needed. Put the entire outfit on including the shoes and walk around. How do the shoes feel? Do you need an insert to keep your shoes from slipping off? Sit down in the outfit in front of a mirror, how does it look? Cross your legs, how does it look? Take a few pictures of yourself in the outfit to see how the ensemble photographs. It always surprises me how differently it can appear.

Getting ready for a big event can be stressful, so go ahead and get your attire ready and feel confident about it. The day of the event you will only need to worry about getting full glam, but the digs are solid!

# DON'T WAIT

Wear the outfit you have been saving for the perfect occasion. Find an excuse to wear it. Don't wait to go on vacation, go to your class reunion, to that party or any other event by making excuses of why you shouldn't.

I had a client who called me a few times and told me she wanted to make an appointment with me for a wardrobe makeover after she lost weight. I had suggested that we should go ahead and do it. She continued to wait. One day she called me and said that she was just going to go ahead and schedule because the diet was not going that well and she wanted to get control of her closet.

I joined her at her home and spent the day clearing out what didn't work for her any longer and put together what did. She tried on clothes for me for several hours and she had a lot of clothes that she was going to donate. She still had so many nice things that fit her very well, but we got out all of the noise. The noise is all of the confusion of clothes that no longer fit her, or compliment her figure. I put together one outfit for each day for one full week. I asked her to please wear that outfit even if she was staying home. Her closet was all set so that she could go to it and know that everything in it fit her. I also showed her how to take basic pieces and add other pieces to it to change up the look as to maximize her outfits.

Several months later, I got a message from her that she had lost a substantial amount of weight. She got a fresh start and felt good about herself in the clothes she already had, plus it was an incentive to take better care of herself and eat better.

I guess the point I am trying to make here is that holding back and waiting isn't doing us any favors in the long run. Take action. Try and appreciate the chapter you are in even if it isn't where you want to stay. You have the ability to turn the page and start a new chapter.

# WEAR A HAT

Hats are fashionable and they also provide nice protection from the sun. Huge and important advice is to wear sunscreen and protect yourself from the rays. It is so damaging to skin. It ages the skin quickly and some people are more prone to skin cancer as well.

I think about all of my years without wearing any sunscreen and being outdoors constantly. I would have liked this advice that I am giving you back then.

Protect your skin. It is your body's best outfit and you want it to look great for years to come.

MOM TO DAUGHTER
AUNT TO NIECE
GRANDMOTHER TO GRANDDAUGHTER
FRIEND TO FRIEND
REMIND ONE ANOTHER

1. YOU ARE IN CHARGE OF YOUR OWN
   HAPPINESS-DON'T RELY ON OTHERS
   TO GIVE IT TO YOU
2. EMOTION IS POWER-FIND YOUR
   PASSION
3. SPEAK UP FOR YOURSELF AND WHAT
   YOU BELIEVE IN
4. TAKE CARE OF YOURSELF. SELF-CARE
   IS NOT BEING SELFISH. SELF-LOVE
5. ACCEPT YOURSELF
6. YOU ARE ENOUGH-YOU ARE SAFE TO
   BE EXACTLY WHO YOU ARE
   DESIGNED TO BE

# Universe ☆

    We are all part of the Universe.
The prefix 'uni' comes from the
Latin ūnus meaning, 'one'.

    So if we are all part of the
UNIverse then we are all part of one
another.

    I am you, you are me –

    Love one another and start
with loving yourself ❤

# Fabulous Notes
# To Self

# Fabulous Notes
# To Self

CPSIA information can be obtained
at www.ICGtesting.com
Printed in the USA
BVHW091740190422
634491BV00002B/63

9 781622 496280